W9-DDA-720

George Washington
A LIFE OF LEADERSHIP

by Robin Nelson

PULL AHEAD BOOKS
Biographies

Lerner Publications Company • Minneapolis

Photo Acknowledgments

The images in this book are used with the permission of: © Bachmann/Photo Network, p. 4; © North Wind Picture Archives, pp. 6, 11, 18, 20; Library of Congress, pp. 8 (LC-USZ62-3913), 12, 14 (LC-USZC4-4971), 16, 23, 25 (LC-DIG-ppmsca-09502), 27 (LC-USZ62-117116); © Historical Picture Archive/CORBIS, p. 10; © Bettmann/CORBIS, p. 17; Independence National Historical Park, p. 19; © SuperStock, p. 22; Erik Kvalsvik for White House Historical Association, p. 24; The Art Archive/Chateau de Blerancourt/Dagli Orti, p. 26. Front Cover: © Museum of the City of New York/CORBIS.

Text copyright © 2006 by Lerner Publications Company

Lerner Publications Company
A division of Lerner Publishing Group
241 First Avenue North
Minneapolis, MN 55401 U.S.A.

Website address: www.lernerbooks.com

Words in **bold type** are explained in a glossary on page 31.

Library of Congress Cataloging-in-Publication Data

Nelson, Robin, 1971–
    George Washington : a life of leadership / by Robin Nelson.
       p. cm. – (Pull ahead books)
    Includes index.
    ISBN-13: 978–0–8225–3474–7 (lib. bdg. : alk. paper)
    ISBN-10: 0–8225–3474–6 (lib. bdg. : alk. paper)
    1. Washington, George, 1732–1799–Juvenile literature. 2. Presidents–United States–Biography–Juvenile literature. I. Title. II. Series.
    E312.66.N45 2006
    973.4'1'092–dc22
                                  2005009039

Manufactured in the United States of America
1 2 3 4 5 6 – JR – 11 10 09 08 07 06

Table of Contents

A Great Leader

Do you know the name of this **monument?** It is the Washington Monument. It is a tower named after George Washington. George Washington was a great **leader.** He was the first president of the United States of America.

George's mother asks him to stay home.

Growing Up

George grew up in Virginia. He **admired** his older brother Lawrence. Lawrence told exciting stories about his sea adventures. George wanted to go to sea. But his mother wanted him to stay close to home.

George fights in the French and Indian War.

The French and Indian War

The countries of Britain and France controlled parts of America. The two countries began to fight over the land. George was a leader in Virginia's army. He asked the French to leave America. They did not leave.

George joined the British army to fight against the French. Some American Indians helped the French. This war was called the French and Indian War.

The British soldiers wore bright red coats and played music as they marched.

The war went on and on. George helped Britain win the war. Britain controlled America.

George Washington, age 25

George leads the American Army.

American Army Leader

Many Americans did not want to be ruled by Britain anymore. George and other American leaders decided that America needed an army to fight the British. George became the leader of the new American army.

The British and American soldiers meet.

The American Revolution

America said it was its own country.
But Britain did not agree. The British
army fought to keep control of America.
The war between Britain and America
was called the **American Revolution.**

The British troops stopped fighting in the winter. It was too cold. But George and his army did not stop.

George and his army try to keep warm in the winter.

One cold night in December, George led his army across an icy river to surprise the British army. George helped his army beat the British!

Soon the British **surrendered** to George and the American army. The British gave up. The Americans won the war. The American Revolution was over. America was free!

George Washington was a hero.

George Washington promises to be a good leader.

President Washington

America became its own country called the United States of America. It needed its own **government.** A government runs a country and creates laws. The United States needed someone to be the leader of the government. The United States needed George Washington.

George Washington became the first president of the United States.

He tried very hard to listen to the needs of all people.

President Washington greets Americans.

George helped to plan the capital city, Washington, D.C. The government would run the country from this city.

The Capitol has grown into a very large city.

George decided what the president's house should look like.

John Adams became the president after George Washington.

George led the country for eight years. Then he decided that it would be better for the country to have a new president.

George Washington was a great leader. He was smart and made good decisions. He was brave, and he listened to others.

GEORGE WASHINGTON TIMELINE

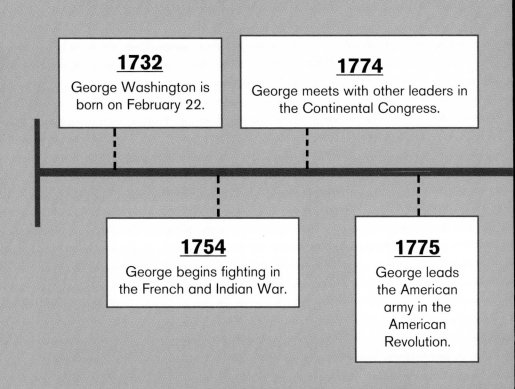

1732
George Washington is born on February 22.

1774
George meets with other leaders in the Continental Congress.

1754
George begins fighting in the French and Indian War.

1775
George leads the American army in the American Revolution.

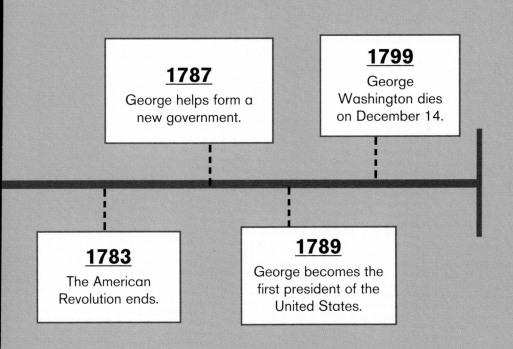

1787
George helps form a
new government.

1799
George
Washington dies
on December 14.

1783
The American
Revolution ends.

1789
George becomes the
first president of the
United States.

More about George Washington

- George Washington is sometimes called the father of our country.

- George Washington was very tall. He was 6 feet 2 inches tall!

- You can see George Washington's face on the dollar bill and the quarter.

Websites

Kids Portrait–George Washington: A National Treasure
http://www.georgewashington.si.edu/kids/portrait.html

US Presidents–George Washington
http://www.whitehouse.gov/kids/presidents/
georgewashington.html

World Almanac for Kids
http://www.worldalmanacforkids.com/explore/presidents/
washington_george.html

Glossary

admired: looked up to

American Revolution: the war between the American colonies and Britain for America's freedom

government: a group of people who run a country

leader: a person who shows the way

monument: something to help people remember a person

surrendered: gave up

Index